Rat-a-tat-tat.
Who is that?
Open the door and see.

Oooh, it's a dragon breathing fire.
He wants to come in for tea.

Oooh, it's a crocodile snapping his teeth.
He wants to come in for tea.

Rat-a-tat-tat.
Who is that?
Open the door and see.

Oooh, it's a monster rolling his eyes.
He wants to come in for tea.

Will I open the door?
Let them in?
Sit them down for tea?

No! No! No!
I don't think so.
They might just gobble up ME!